Manga

by David Orme

Trailblazers

Manga

by David Orme
Educational consultant: Helen Bird

Illustrated by Peter Richardson

Published by Ransom Publishing Ltd.
Rose Cottage, Howe Hill, Watlington, Oxon. OX49 5HB
www.ransom.co.uk

ISBN   184167 593 8
         978 184167 593 0

First published in 2006

Manga

Contents

Manga

Get the facts

What is Manga?

Comic books for teenagers and adults started in the **USA** in the **1930s**.

Manga comics started in **Japan** in the **1950s**.

They were a mixture of traditional Japanese drawing and American comics.

The characters were drawn in a special way.

Many of them had big eyes.

Astroboy – an early Manga character

Manga themes

At first Manga was for children.

Later comics had themes
that teenagers liked:

- **Science fiction**
- **Horror**
- **Fantasy**
- **Love stories**
- **Samurai** and **Ninja**
  stories.

In the **1980s** Manga
became popular in the
USA and Europe. The
language was changed
from **Japanese** to **English**.

Manga is still very popular in Japan. There are even
non-fiction and school books that use Manga.

People also love Manga films!
They are called **Animé**.

Pokemon Manga

Pokemon stands for
Pocket Monsters.
Pokemon is a video
game series.

Many of the monsters and other
characters are based on Manga.

7

Samurai and Ninja

Who were the Samurai?

The story of the Samurai goes back over 1,000 years.

Japan was run by local chiefs. The Samurai were their warriors. They kept law and order.

The Samurai had a special code. They had to fight fairly. For a Samurai, being good at studying was just as important as being good at fighting.

The Samurai lasted until 1877. After that there was a Japanese army for the whole country.

Ninja

The Samurai were real people in the history of Japan.

There were real people who called themselves Ninja, but most of the stories about them are made up.

People say they came from poor families who were not allowed to become Samurai.

Ninja means '***People who do things quietly***'.

The Ninja were not open and fair like the Samurai. They wore black clothes and were good at sneaking up on people in the dark.

Boffin Boy

v.

Mogon

the

Mighty

Chapter 1:
Mogon the Mighty

A storm was raging on a high mountain. Heavy rain pushed rocks and earth down the mountain side. Where the rocks had been, something was sticking out of the ground.

A metal hand!

It was Mogon, a mighty robot built centuries ago.

A storm was raging.

This was the hand of Mogon the Mighty!

Dang Po was Mogon's builder. He had made the robot so he could rule the world. But something had gone wrong. Mogon would not obey his master. He wanted to rule Earth himself!

There was a long and bitter battle. At last, Mogon had been defeated. He had been buried in a pit on the top of a high mountain.

Now, thousands of years later, wind and rain had washed the top of the mountain away.

ang Po had built the robot thousands
years ago.
ut it would not
bey him.

Chapter 2:
Power!

The storm became fiercer. A great bolt of lightning struck the metal arm.

Power!

Slowly, the earth began to move.

At last, the mighty Mogon, killer of all living things, stood tall and proud on the mountain top.

Lightning flashed again, striking Mogon's head.

More power!

Mogon's legs began to move.

He set off down the mountain.

He was very, very, angry.

Chapter 3:
Boffin Boy

Far away, in a big house in a secret valley, Rick Shaw was talking to his mother.

It was a sad day. Rick's father had just been buried. He had died in an accident in his secret laboratory.

Rick had worked with his father. When he was younger, he had been sent to school, but he had been too clever even for his teachers. He had been called 'Boffin Boy'. Rick didn't care what people called him. He was only interested in science. He had left school. He came home to work with his father.

"Now your father's work will never be finished!" Rick's mother said sadly.

"Yes it will! I know as much as father did. I will finish his work!"

"But Rick, you are so young!"

"What does that matter? I am **Boffin Boy**!"

Now your father is dead, his work will never be finished.
I will finish it! I am **BOFFIN BOY**!

Just then the phone rang. Rick answered it.

"It's the government, mother! A huge robot from the past has just trashed Tokyo! They wanted father's help to destroy it!"

Rick spoke on the phone.

"My father is dead. But don't worry. I am his son. I will do all I can!"

"Rick, don't even think about it! I don't want to lose you as well!"

"I am sorry Mother, but the world needs me. The world needs Boffin Boy!"

The phone rings.
A huge robot is destroying the world.
I will do all I can!
Oh no! I don't want to lose you as well!
But the world needed Boffin Boy!

Chapter 4:
The World is destroyed - well, almost

Nothing could stop Mogon the Mighty. People thought he would be trapped in Japan, but the robot was clever. He made himself wings, and a jet pack for his back. He could go anywhere in the world.

He hated human beings. He wanted a world where only robots lived. Every human, every animal, every plant, would be destroyed.

Mogon learnt to fly . . .

He wanted to destroy every living thing.

Rick Shaw's powerful brain took in the reports from all over the world. He soon worked out what the armies of the world were doing wrong.

"If you drop a bomb on him, or fire a laser beam, it makes things worse! He needs power to keep going. His body stores up the power from the weapons!"

"So what can we do? Anyway, what do you know? You're just a kid!"

Boffin Boy soon worked out what the armies were doing wrong . . .
What do you know? You're just a kid!
The weapons are giving him his power!

"No I'm not! Well, yes, I am, but remember, I'm Boffin Boy! And I'm going to set him a trap!"

At first the leaders of the world took no notice. But Mogon carried on destroying things. At last they agreed to Rick's daring plan.

I am **BOFFIN BOY!**

And I'm going to set a trap for Mogon!

Chapter 5:
The secret books of Wu Pee

On a secret island in the South China Sea, the brilliant Doctor Wu Pee was reading his old books. Somewhere there must be a way to defeat The Mighty Mogon.

He cried out in delight. "I have found it!"

Minutes later, Wu Pee talked to Rick Shaw by video link.

"I have found the records of the great Dang Po. I know the secret call sign he used to make the robot come to him."

"Wu Pee! That's just what I need for my trap!"

Chapter 6:
The pit of doom

The trap was ready. It was a huge pit lined with steel. Next to it was a radio station. Rick started to send the secret call sign.

Across the world, the Mighty Mogon stopped wrecking things. The call sign! Dang Po must still be alive! The man he hated most!

The trap was ready. Boffin Boy had made a huge pit . . .

Now to send the call sign!

And Mogon heard it . . .

My call sign! Dang Po must be alive!

I will kill him!

With a roar of fury he leapt into the air. He followed the signals to the pit.

"Where are you, Dang Po?" roared Mogon. "Prepare to die!"

"I am here, Mogon. In the pit!"

Mogon flew into the mighty pit. But something was wrong.

"You're not Dang Po! You are . . .

Where are you, Dang Po?
Prepare to die!
I am here, in the pit.
Mogon followed the signals to the pit . . . He flew into the pit.

"Boffin Boy!" roared Rick. "And I have you in my power!"

Rick threw a switch. The great machines he had invented started to suck the power out of the robot.

Soon, the Mighty Mogon was just a heap of rusty metal.

Manga word check

characters	robot
chiefs	Samurai
code	science
comic	science fiction
government	sneaking
Japanese	studying
laboratory	superheroes
lightning	traditional
mountain	warriors
Ninja	weapons
Pokemon	wizards
popular	